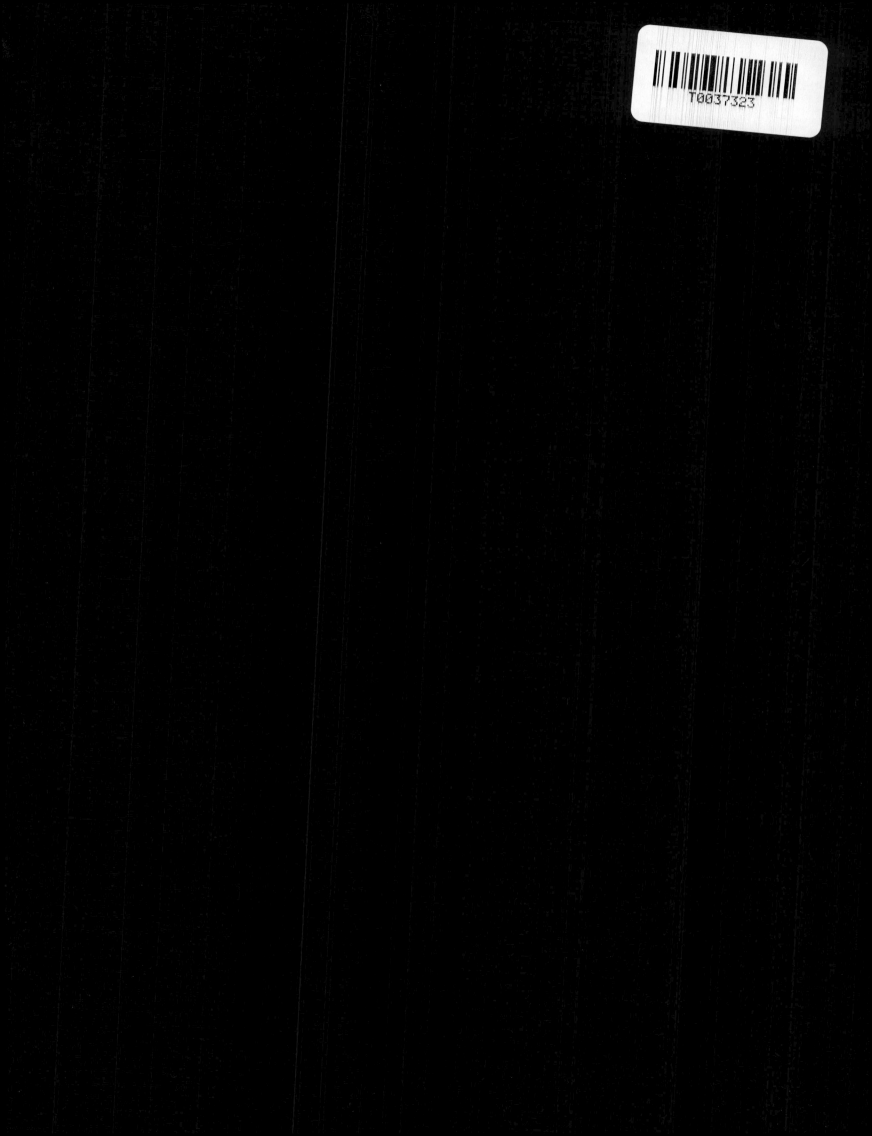

MINECRAFT™
EPIC INVENTIONS

BUILDS TO SPARK YOUR IMAGINATION

NEW YORK

Copyright © 2022 by Mojang AB. All Rights Reserved. Minecraft, the MINECRAFT logo and the MOJANG STUDIOS logo are trademarks of the Microsoft group of companies.

Published in the United States by Del Rey, an imprint of Random House, a division of Penguin Random House LLC, New York.

DEL REY and the CIRCLE colophon are registered trademarks of Penguin Random House LLC.

Originally published in hardcover in the United Kingdom by Farshore, an imprint of HarperCollins Publishers Limited.

ISBN 978-0-593-49764-7
Ebook ISBN 978-0-593-49765-4

Printed in the United States on acid-free paper

randomhousebooks.com

2 4 6 8 9 7 5 3 1

First US Edition

Written by Thomas McBrien
Illustrations by Swampbaron

CONTENTS

ROXY ROCKET, ENGINEER

Hi! Hello! Over here! Sorry I can't be with you in person today, but I'm currently thousands of blocks away in outer space. We'll meet later on when you visit my intergalactic space station, *The Pathfinder*.

PER PLEX, GAME SHOW HOST

My name is Persephone, but you can call me Per. Are you feeling lucky? I've built the realm's one and only game show and I'm inviting you to come try your chances at my games. I'm hoping they'll leave you feeling perplexed!

PRINCESS SKY, KAWAII SPECIALIST

Come visit my kawaii paradise high in the sky, where I've created the best waterway course in all the world. It's got kitty cats, flying pigs, baby chicks – all the cutest animals. Join me for a race through my magical waterways.

GLADICE ATOR, GAMES MASTER

I'm looking for champions. Only the bestest, strongest, nimblest players in the realm need visit my build. If that's you, come to my arena and prove yourself to the realm.

DEN PORTALWALKER, INTERDIMENSIONAL SCIENTIST

Sleep? SLEEP? Who needs sleep?! I grew up in the Nether. While my fellow builders slept in comfy beds, I didn't sleep at all! This gave me endless time to pursue my main interest: science. My inventions are for scientific research.

WOLFGANG CLAWHAUSER, ZOOLOGIST

Welcome to the Animal Sanctuary! Shhh! Keep your voice down – we don't want to disturb the mobs. I'm the group's zoologist, and my creations are for the welfare of mobs. I've created homes for all of Minecraft's friendly mobs in my animal sanctuary.

INTRODUCTION

Welcome to the Creator's Realm! This realm is the creative center of the universe, where expert inventors come to create and test all their latest inventions. If it's possible to imagine it, these folks can make it! All the inventors you meet today are the best in the biz. Let's say hello and hear all about their top tips and tricks.

PROF. FIONA FIXER, RESTORATION EXPERT

What do I do? My background is in antiquities, but my specialty is restoration. I've been tinkering with gadgets since I found my first redstone dust, so if anyone can get an old machine up and running again, it's me.

TOPSY TURVY, AERIAL ENGINEER

Have you ever played in an amplified world? I've built my creation on the underside of an amplified mountain arch. It provides the best view in the realm!

DR. NEFARIOUS, EVIL MASTERMIND

Ever dreamed of having a place in the sun? Take a trip to my resort island, Skull Mountain, where there's more to this build than meets the eye.

FRANKIE EINSTEIN, DIABOLICAL GENIUS

Come visit me in my Gothic castle, where I have been experimenting with the creation of life itself. My invention is a house of horrors!

MIKE ROSCOPIC, MEEPLE DESIGNER

Hi, I'm Mike and I put the mini in mini-people. Or meeple, as they're affectionately known. All my inventions are for overcoming size-related hurdles in my oversized bedroom world.

CLINT WESTWARD, COWBOY INVENTOR

Howdy! As they say, some cowboys have too much tumbleweed in their blood to settle down – and I've some of that old grit in me. Come visit me in my traveling saloon for a drink to quench your thirst.

GENERAL REDSTONE TIPS

You too could be an expert inventor. All it takes is a little practice and a small dose of imagination! I know that getting used to the redstone mechanics can be challenging, so I'm here with my fellow expert inventors to share some of our top tips, so that you too can create epic inventions. You'll see just what you can create when you follow these tips and marvel at our inventions.

GETTING STARTED   1

CREATIVE MODE
Playing in Creative mode will give you the power to build to your heart's desire with unlimited access to all the blocks in the game at your fingertips. If you're looking for a real challenge, though, you can play in Survival mode, but if you're trying a new project, we recommend playing in Creative mode.

REDSTONE BLOCKS
There are dozens of redstone blocks and items you can play with in Minecraft, and each of them works in a unique way. It's important to first be familiar with them before you start making redstone inventions. Begin by placing them in the world and seeing what they do.

TUTORIALS
There are many tutorials available that you can follow to learn more about redstone. There are even a few in this book! Try following these tutorials to quickly learn the basics of redstone mechanisms.

REDSTONE SIGNALS

Redstone signals have a maximum power of 15. This means that an output signal can travel up to 15 blocks away before it vanishes. If you need to send a signal farther, you can use a redstone repeater to boost the signal back to full charge.

IDEAS

Once you know how the redstone blocks and items work, you can begin working on your inventions. Start out small and slowly develop your ideas over time. Most big inventions are actually composed of many small, simple mechanisms.

3 IMPROVING

TESTING

Building your first invention will likely take some time. Start by breaking your idea down to its core elements and try to build each part independently. When each part works, look to see if you can merge them together to make a more powerful invention.

UPGRADING

When you finish your first invention, it will likely be a chunky, messy build. That's totally fine – if it works, it works! Now it's time to see if you can improve your design. The best redstone inventors know lots of tricks for simplifying their work.

ANIMAL SANCTUARY

When I was younger, I roamed the Overworld, climbing to the tops of mountains and diving to the depths of oceans in search of the wildlife that inhabits our world. Until one day, I found myself lost in a barren land of dead bushes and terracotta – somewhere no mob could call home. So I set out to change that and used my years of zoology experience to build this safe haven for mobs.

MOB HOSPITAL
A hospital and research facility dedicated to the welfare of mobs. This is the main hub of our mob care and conservation program.

SNOW QUARTER
A cool place for cold-biome mobs such as polar bears.

WOLFGANG CLAWHAUSER
ZOOLOGIST

12

SANCTUARY TOWERS

JUNGLE

CAVE ENTRANCE
Some of our mob friends, such as axolotls, prefer to live underground.

SANCTUARY ENTRANCE

FORCEFIELD EMITTER
Tall forcefields keep unwanted and hostile intruders outside the animal sanctuary.

INVENTIVE DETAILS

I consulted my travel diaries to find out what my sanctuary needed. For mobs to thrive, they must have suitable homes, food and caretakers. And above all, they need protection when the sun goes down.

MOB HOSPITAL

My first build was the mob hospital. Transporting mobs is challenging, so I brought them here in pairs and bred them to increase their numbers. It's not an animal sanctuary unless you have lots of mobs to fill it with!

SANCTUARY TOWERS

Some of our inhabitants don't get along, so we need to keep an eye on them from towers to make sure they stay apart. The ladder is placed against flipped-up trapdoors to make it as thin as possible.

FARM

On the farm, my villagers grow everything the mobs could need, from carrots and beetroot to dandelions and wheat. I placed some composters, so the villagers can help take care of the land.

BEE HABITAT

Bees are vital for ecosystems, helping to pollinate the plants which, in turn, support so many mobs. This habitat is the secret to the success of my sanctuary. There are plenty of flowers and bee nests around to keep them buzzing along.

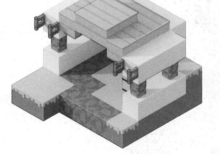

MARINE SANCTUARY

This body of water is for our underwater friends. Lighting up underwater spaces is difficult but essential to ensure hostile mobs can't hang around, so I built a conduit.

HORSE STABLE

Horses are happy mobs, apart from when a storm comes – then they'll need a shelter. I added hay bales inside to keep them fed and fences to tether them to.

BLOCK CHOICES

The animal sanctuary is an incredibly diverse space, so that all the mobs can feel at home. I've used hundreds of different blocks, but here are some of the main ones I used for the buildings.

sandstone

smooth sandstone

red sandstone

stripped oak log

15

INVENTIVE DETAILS

Mobs thrive best when left undisturbed. While I knew some villagers would be needed to tend to the land, I decided to create inventions that would limit how many of them I'd need. This enclosure is for mobs!

RESEARCH CENTER

Inside the hospital, we conduct our humane research on the mobs. We've discovered lots of fascinating behaviors. Did you know that the allay loves to collect items? These happy mobs help us bring food to hungry animals.

FORCEFIELD EMITTER

To help keep this sanctuary free from outside interference – both the hostile and the curious – these forcefield emitters generate a powerful wall around the perimeter.

VILLAGER HOUSING

Villagers are the perfect caretakers. Once given a job, they'll do it without hesitation. These houses are built to blend into the wilderness of the sanctuary, with walls of dirt and discreet daylight sensors to power the lights.

MOB FEEDER

This invention is simple but effective. Hungry mobs just head over to their favorite food dispenser and step on a pressure plate to activate it. Every time they step on the dispenser, they'll be given another treat.

MOB FEEDER MECHANISM DETAIL

SCIENCE TOWER

Ah, my primary residence! This is the most advanced part of my build and where I make all my inventions, such as my mob feeder and water trough.

AUTOMATIC WATER TROUGH

This invention utilizes the most powerful energy source in the world: the sun! The trough empties at night and refills with water when the sun rises.

MONSTER FACTORY

Boo! Aha, if that scared you, maybe you should skip ahead to the next build. This is the spookiest place in the realm. It's where horrors are born! No, not born. Created. That's right, my great invention is the stuff of nightmares: its a factory for the supernatural. I've harnessed the power of storms to bring my terrifying monsters to life! Why? Because I can!

INFERNAL GATE

GARDENS
A supply minecart brings fresh food from the gardens to the kitchen – monsters can get very hungry!

QUARRY
A mine for coal and iron – the resources I need to run my factory.

PUMPKIN FARM

STORM CATCHER
This copper rod catches lightning strikes to power my monster factory.

GREAT HALL

HALL OF HORRORS
This is where I keep my wicked invention: a redstone factory for creating iron golems!

FRANKIE EINSTEIN
DIABOLICAL GENIUS

ENCHANTING TOWER

I collected all the books I could find to create this library. I can enchant the most powerful weapons for my creatures of the night to wield.

My monster factory is built inside a Gothic castle. These tall walls keep my projects safe from prying eyes, and the high ceilings give my precious monsters the space they need to roam around.

STAINED-GLASS WINDOW

The large windows are made using purple stained glass and tinted glass. My castle houses many undead mobs and the tinted glass allows them to walk around inside during the day.

BUTTRESSES

The castle walls reach over 70 blocks tall. These interior and exterior buttresses provide extra support to the heavy load, and help give the structure a Gothic style.

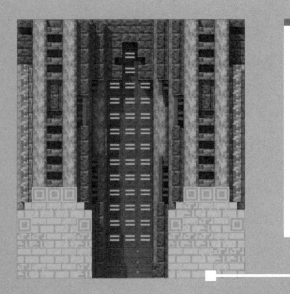

GRAND ENTRANCE

Although there are few visitors to my castle, I like to make a good first impression on those who do stop by. This imposing grand entrance lets everyone know I am not to be trifled with!

SPIKY TOWER

This tall, imposing tower can be seen from far away. The red glow of redstone torches gives the structure an ominous vibe.

PUMPKIN FARM

My golems require carved pumpkins to come to life. I grow the pumpkins myself and use shears to carve them, then feed the seeds to the composter for bone meal.

BLOCK CHOICES

I wanted a foreboding, Gothic style for my castle, so I used a lot of stone and light-producing blocks to create this vibe.

deepslate tiles

stone bricks

polished basalt

purple stained glass

lanterns

INFERNAL ENTRANCE

This is the first line of defense for my castle. Anyone who dares launch an assault on my home will first need to get through these thick defensive walls. The wide walkway has space for dozens of skeleton archers.

STORM CATCHER

The storm catcher is the tallest point of my build, and at the very tip is a copper rod. This rod harnesses the energy of storms to power my monster factory. When lightning strikes, a redstone signal is sent to activate my golem maker! How awesome is that?

Here is the heart of my build: the golem maker. I've invented a contraption capable of creating iron golems. It runs on the unstoppable power of nature!

GOLEM MAKER

Iron golems are made using iron blocks and carved pumpkins. This ingenious contraption uses redstone to build the creatures and bring them to life.

HOW IT WORKS

To use the iron golem maker, you will need to place an iron block on all four of the piston faces and keep the dispenser stocked with carved pumpkins. Press the button to activate the pistons and say hello to your new iron golem!

1

Make a line of concrete blocks with 4 branches as shown, and add 2 blocks on the opposite side of the third branch. Add 2 blocks to the outer branches in a stair formation and join the central branches, adding an extra block on one side as shown.

2

Continue building the support structure, adding 2 blocks to each of the outer stairs and 4 blocks to the center as shown.

3

Place redstone dust along each branch, connecting them at the bottom.

4

Place 7 redstone repeaters and adjust the tick speed so that the two in the middle are set to 4 and all others are set to 1 as shown. Then add a button at the front of the build.

7

Finally, decorate the maker with your chosen theme. Place 4 iron blocks, one on each of the piston faces. Fill the chest with iron blocks.

5

Add 6 pistons facing the center of the build as shown. These will push the pieces of your golem together.

6

Place a dispenser at the top and fill it with carved pumpkins.

KAWAII WATERWAYS

I hope you brought your towel because we're about to embark on the wildest ride of your life! My inventions are inspired by my one true aspiration: having fun! This build is one big waterway race, packed with everything from gravity-defying waterfalls and boat bouncers to rainbow bridges and even fireworks. These waterways will test the mettle of even the most skilled racers.

BOAT BOUNCER
Launch across to the next waterway with the boat bouncer!

FINISH LINE
The first to cross the line is greeted with an epic fireworks display.

KITTY CAT SHRINE

STARTING LINE
Get in your boats and ride!

FLYING PIGS

REVERSE WATERFALL
A gravity-defying waterfall – contestants go up the waterfall instead of down.

RAINBOW BRIDGE

PRINCESS SKY
KAWAII SPECIALIST

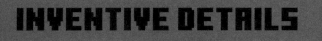

I styled my waterways on the cutest animal in the kingdom: kawaii cats. These majestic animals keep a close eye on everything you do – so no cheating! They also bestow gifts to their favorite players.

CAT SHRINE

All hail our mighty rulers! These decorative cat shrines are made using banners and concrete. They overlook the starting and finish lines, and make sure no one cheats!

FLYING PIGS

I love pink and I love animals. So, naturally, I had to have both in my build – like these flying pink pigs. Oink! So adorable.

STARTING LINE

On your marks, climb into your boats, get set ... GO! This is where the race starts. Choose your starting position carefully: Players at the front will be in the lead but may get bumped around by the players behind.

white wool

white concrete

pink wool

pink concrete

water

RAINBOW FINISH LINE

It's an uphill race to reach the finish line. Bumping into players will be twice as punishing here! It's a chance to catch up to first place, but there's also a risk of falling into last.

BLOCK CHOICES

My waterways are packed with all the colors of the rainbow. Using a mixture of wool and concrete in mostly white and pink, I built the clouds and trees. And don't forget the most important block: water!

SPECTATOR STANDS

Spectators can watch the race from these stands. The high vantage point will give them a clear view of the waterways, and spyglasses can be used to keep a close eye on the action.

RAINBOW BRIDGE

Look out for this rainbow bridge ahead – once you cross it, you'll know you're near the finish line and running out of time to reach first place. It's time to paddle at full speed!

INVENTIVE DETAILS

My waterways float high in the sky on big white clouds. There are multiple routes you can take, each one connected by one of my waterway inventions.

FLOATING CLOUD

These floating clouds form the structures for the waterways. They're made using white concrete and white wool, and the trees are made of pink concrete and pink wool. Everything is illuminated by floating glowstone.

REVERSE WATERFALL

This isn't your regular waterfall – it pulls players upstream instead of letting them fall down! The soul sand at the base creates a bubble column that raises players to the next stretch of water.

WATERWAY EXTENSION PISTON BRIDGE

The extension bridge links two of the waterway sections, using tripwires and pistons. As you paddle your boat across, tripwires trigger sticky pistons to keep you from falling. Watch out that your competitors don't bump you to the side though!

WATERWAY FEATURES

Racers never get bored of competing on my kawaii waterway. There are multiple ways to get to the finish line, each as challenging as the other. You can choose between perilous drops, island jumps and reverse waterfalls. There's even a piston bridge to paddle across! Let's take a look at some of these obstacles.

BRIDGE ISLAND

Build your momentum to cross the extension bridge quickly.

ISLAND FALL

Drop from one cloud to the next in this perilous fall!

SECTION OF JUMP ISLAND

JUMP ISLAND

Take time to position your boat carefully! There's a piston to throw you to the next island, but miss it and you'll lose time doubling back.

ISLAND SPLITTER

Choose your route carefully! Each has its own hazards.

PARANORMAL FACILITY

Good, you made it through the portal in one piece. Welcome to the lab! This research facility has been built to pioneer research across two dimensions: the Nether and the Overworld. Here we can see the Nether side of the operation, where I built labs for research and development. There's a lot of experiments going on, so please do not press any buttons.

RESEARCH LABS

LAVA PIT
Sometimes my creations are too unstable to keep stored away – that's when they get thrown into the lava to be destroyed before anything can go wrong.

BACKUP GENERATOR
In case of a ghast attack, the backup generator ensures our experiments keep running even if the main generator is damaged.

DEN PORTALWALKER
INTERDIMENSIONAL SCIENTIST

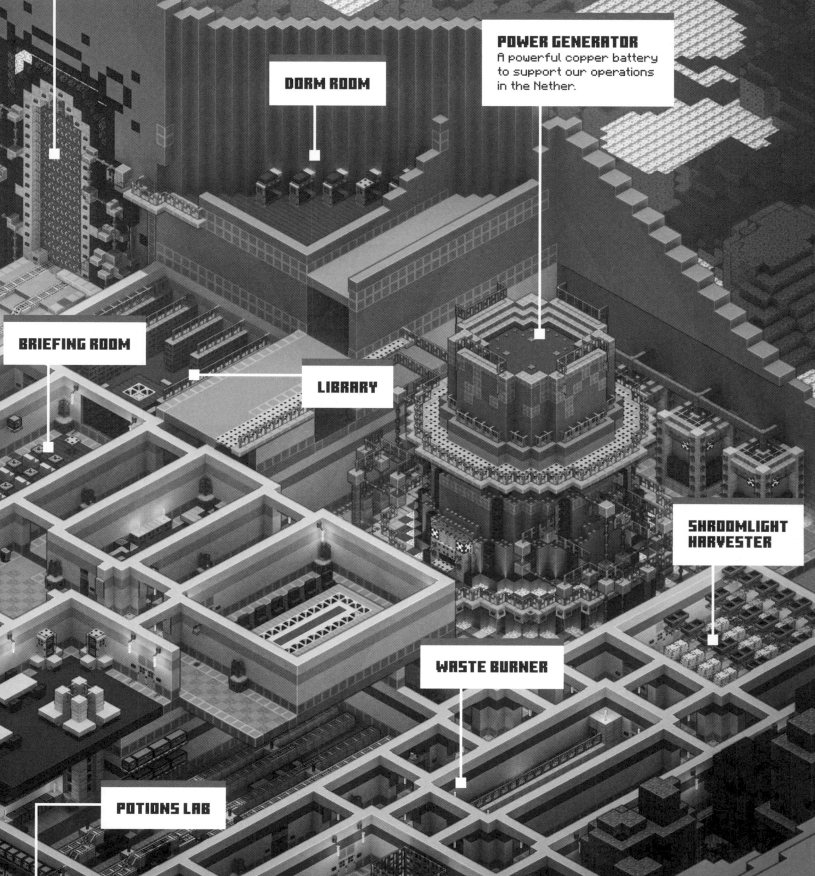

INTERDIMENSIONAL PORTAL
This supersized portal allows for interdimensional experimentation. Make sure never to touch a minecart before it has been decontaminated!

DORM ROOM

POWER GENERATOR
A powerful copper battery to support our operations in the Nether.

BRIEFING ROOM

LIBRARY

SHROOMLIGHT HARVESTER

WASTE BURNER

POTIONS LAB

Cleanliness is of the utmost importance in the pursuit of science. That's why white and gray blocks are used throughout my builds, so anything amiss will quickly be spotted.

BRIEFING ROOM

I've made lots of discoveries in the Nether. This room is where I share them with fellow scientists. Shared knowledge is shared power.

POTIONS LAB

Safety first! Whether it's drinking a Potion of Fire Resistance before studying the effects of lava or a Potion of Strength to open that really tight jar lid, potions can be of incredible value to the pursuit of science. The dispensers are for distributing essential potions.

BLOCK CHOICES

The research at this facility is of the utmost importance. We cannot take any risks! Each zone is designated with a color scheme to signify the type of activity within.

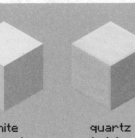

yellow concrete

RESEARCH CELLS AND LAB

The best practice when testing new materials is to keep them isolated. These cells are secured with iron doors, and before leaving the lab, you must first shower in the decontamination unit.

white concrete

quartz bricks

smooth stone

green concrete

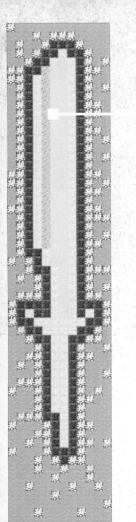

SWORD MOSAIC

Made out of gold and raw gold blocks, surrounded by blackstone and shroomlight, this sword is the symbol of the organization that runs this facility, made massive on the ground for decoration.

CORROSIVE SUBSTANCES LAB

After an unfortunate incident with gunpowder, I decided to create a special lab for corrosive substances. This lab has a fire-resistant room for testing new potions that may cause unexpected damage. The gray-and-yellow concrete warns visitors not to step too close.

POWER GENERATOR

This huge copper battery is central to my Nether lab. The acid fluids inside are contained behind iron blocks and iron bars, and the copper has been waxed to ensure it does not corrode over time. It is then encased in protective layers of water and obsidian to avoid contaminating the ground.

INVENTIVE DETAILS

This build is packed with all the latest technology, including some of my very own inventions. I've taken extra precautions to defend against both scientific mishaps and hostile intruders.

BATTERY POWER SOURCE

The power generator stores energy in these batteries, which feeds out to support experiments throughout the facility. The volatile energy is safely contained behind blackstone and iron blocks. You must switch 56 levers to turn it off, so there's no risk of it happening by accident.

VINE ROOM

Sourcing vines has been a mortal challenge for my staff – those pesky piglins are a nuisance! This automatic vine farm produces all the vines we need. I'll soon be adding a lava farm using a similar model, with dripstone and cauldrons.

DOUBLE PISTON EXTENDER

In case of emergency, these double piston extenders will activate to seal the lab doors and block holding-cell exits, so that nothing can escape.

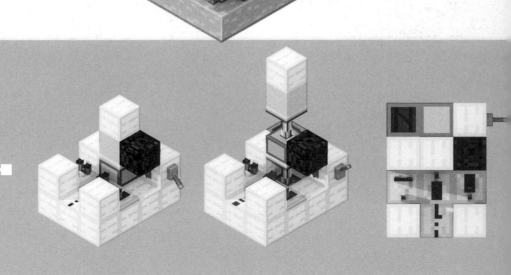

NETHER TRANSPORT HUB

This interdimensional portal allows for travel between the Overworld and the Nether. A set of minecart rails lead in and out of the portal for carrying experiments to be conducted in both dimensions.

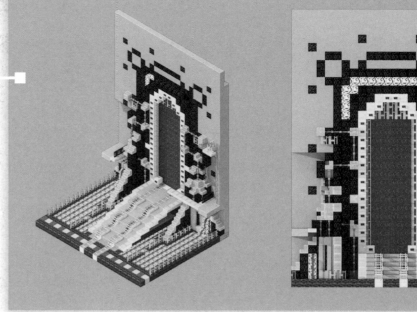

SECURITY CAMERAS

The hallways are lined with security cameras to ensure no intruders can wander around unnoticed. We can't risk a dangerous substance falling into the wrong hands!

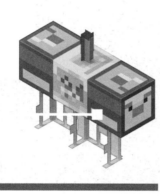

DISPOSAL UNIT

Each of the labs is connected to a disposal unit. However, when big experiments go terribly wrong, it's best to dump them into the lava.

DEFENSE BARRIER

Several ranks of defense barriers are positioned in front of the Nether portal. If pillagers ever come through the portal, we're set to keep them at bay here.

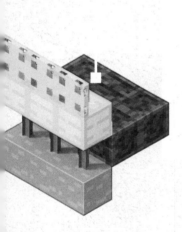

BACKUP POWER GENERATOR

The backup generator is a crude system that uses thermal sources to extract power. It's a costly system to run, but an essential fail-safe in case anything were to happen to the main generator. If the lights ever go out, the daylight sensor activates the backup generator so that experiments continue uninterrupted.

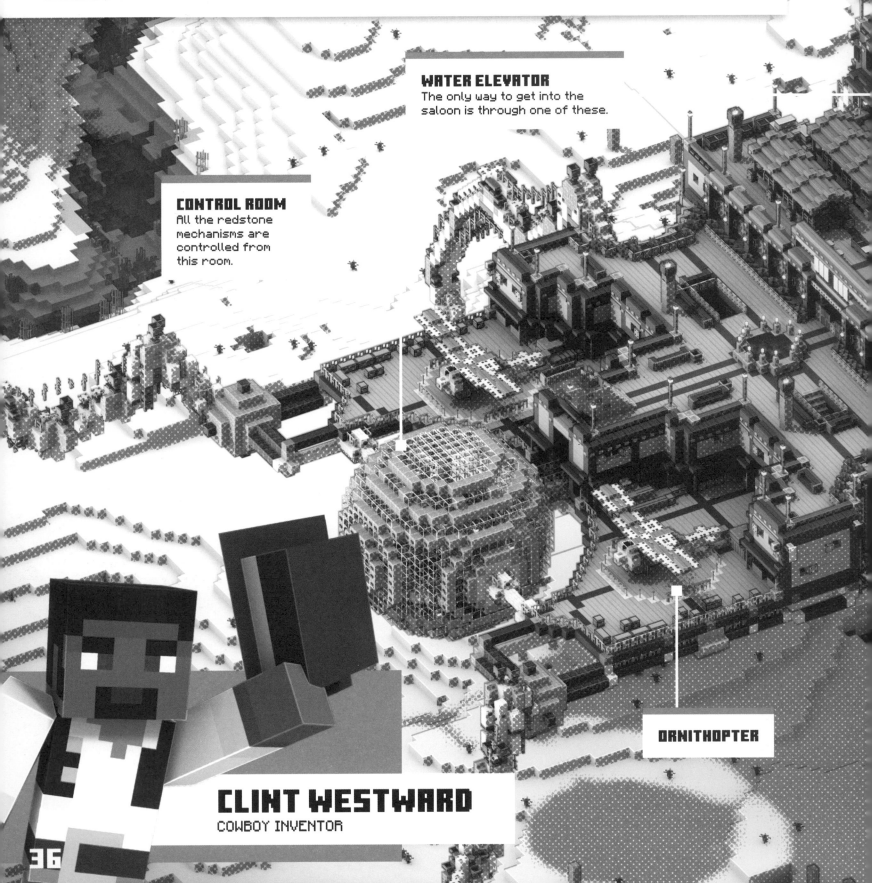

EIGHT-LEGGED SALOON

Yeehaw! Giddy up yer horses and clamber aboard. Quick as you can now, this watering hole is always on the move and isn't it a sight for sore eyes? It's a rootin' tootin' walkin' saloon! My marvelous invention is pushing the western frontier even farther west — there ain't no mountain too high or river too deep to stop my journey.

WATER ELEVATOR
The only way to get into the saloon is through one of these.

CONTROL ROOM
All the redstone mechanisms are controlled from this room.

ORNITHOPTER

CLINT WESTWARD
COWBOY INVENTOR

BAND PAVILION

TERRACE SEATING
This dining area allows my patrons to watch the world go by while they have a refreshing drink or two.

STABLES

MECHANICAL LEGS
These legs allow the saloon to walk where it pleases.

Taming the temper of this beast requires more effort than your average horse. The mechanics need tender love and care. The bigger challenge, however, is keeping the residents from becoming too rowdy!

MECHANICAL LEG

The saloon is supported by eight mechanical spider legs, hoisting the build over 30 blocks into the air.

BUNKHOUSE

A series of bunkhouses provide beds for over a hundred patrons. Depending on how your gold rush is going, you can either pay to stay in your own penthouse or share a bunkroom with a dozen other people.

BAND PAVILION

Nothing gets my patrons in a merry mood quite like a good jig! I employ only the best musicians, as my fellow riders are known to be picky and will express their dislike with a well-aimed egg throw.

STABLES

Stables provide housing for all manner of mounts — horses, donkeys, mules, even pigs. Each stable comes with complimentary food and a trough.

CONTROL SPHERE

All mechanisms are connected to the control-sphere lever panels, from the water elevator entrance to the mechanical legs. Even the dunking stool has a control in case no one hits the target quickly enough.

ORNITHOPTER

This build features two ornithopters. While I endeavor to have everything anyone could possibly want in my supply chests, if I am ever lacking a resource, I rush out on one of the ornithopters to go get it.

INVENTIVE DETAILS

Traveling on an ever-moving spider makes it tricky to pick up passengers, but more challenging is enticing them to stay and come along for the ride! I've come up with plenty of cool inventions to make this THE saloon in the Wild West.

PISTON TABLE AND KEGS

I've created tables using pistons, redstone torches and carpets. The barrels are filled with drinks for the patrons.

DUNKING STOOL

The dunking stool is a classic form of entertainment in the Wild West. Act a fool and you'll be placed on the trapdoor. Patrons can then take turns trying to hit the target block and make you fall into the water.

SMOKE STACKS

Between the redstone engines, campfires and fireworks shooting off every few minutes, there's a lot of smoke in the common areas. These smoke stacks keep the saloon's air nice and fresh.

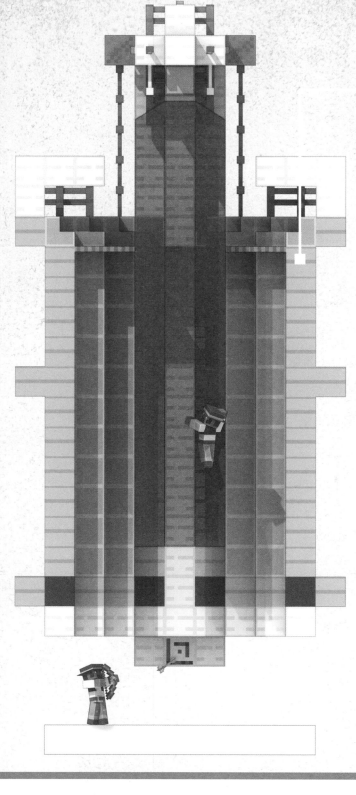

WATERFALL ELEVATOR

You've got to be a sharp shooter to get into this saloon! The only entrance is through the waterfall elevators. Pull out your bow and take aim – you must hit the target block, which will then trigger water to flow from the top of the tower, creating a channel for you to swim up and into the belly of the spider.

BLOCK CHOICES

This walking saloon has been built to look like an old Western saloon in the shape of an insect with large mechanical legs; therefore, I used a mix of wood and metal blocks for my build.

oxidized cut copper

iron blocks

iron bars

oak planks

campfires

SIGNAL LADDER

The target block is connected to a redstone torch signal ladder. Once hit, the target block will send a signal up the ladder to activate the dispenser.

41

TEMPLE OF WONDERS

Welcome to the jungle! This temple is the biggest discovery I've ever made and the greatest restoration project of my career. I've been working tirelessly to bring these ancient ruins back to functioning order. It's astonishing what my ancestors were able to invent. Don't let its beautiful exterior fool you – the temple's interiors are full of booby traps! Watch where you stand.

TEMPLE BALCONIES

COVERED WALKWA
These walkways provid
shelter from the ever-
present spray from th
many waterfalls.

MEETING CIRCLE
An altar sits in the center of the structure.

GREAT LAKES

PROF. FIONA FIXER
RESTORATION EXPERT

AQUEDUCT

MAIN TEMPLE COMPLEX
The temple burrows back and down into the mountain, with balconies and outlets along the mountain's edge.

TEMPLE WALLS
Walls are hidden within the dense jungle to make sure would-be temple robbers are forced to take the path lined with traps.

SPOOKY TOWERS
Skull-lined towers run through the forest alongside the aqueduct.

BANYAN TREE FOREST

INVENTIVE DETAILS

My ancestors built their city around an enormous banyan tree. The roots are massive and capable of supporting a series of stone structures and a deep network of tunnels.

MEETING CIRCLE

A stone ring has been built around the trunk of the largest banyan tree, with entrances leading in every direction. It must have been some kind of ceremonial temple, as within the structure are steps leading to an altar.

AQUEDUCT

A colossal aqueduct carries a stream of water through the forest. I wonder what it was there for — could the original builders have used it for the transport of goods? The tiered structure of the aqueduct suggests they may have.

CAVE NETWORK

The structure stretches deep underground, through a network of built-up caves. The use of deepslate blocks suggests they ventured far, far below ground. Some of the structures also use blackstone! Perhaps they were the creators of the now-ruined portals?

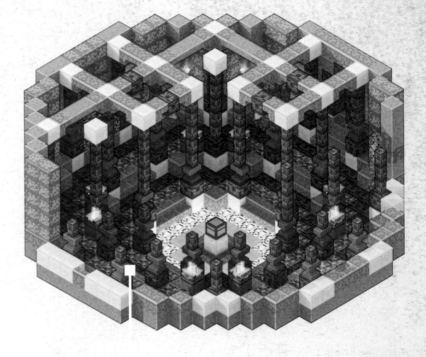

TREASURE ROOM

The cave network leads to this underground treasure room carved into a deepslate gold-ore deposit. At the center is a trapped chest linked to another deadly booby trap.

TEMPLE OF WONDERS TOWERS

These temples give a dark, foreboding aura as you pass them, and the spore blossoms by the entrances fill the air with a strange green fog. Inside, skulls hang from the walls, marking the graves of all the ancient generations who lived here before – incredible!

stone bricks | mossy stone bricks | cobblestone | deepslate | birch slabs

BLOCK CHOICES

This jungle temple has been built with blocks from the surrounding area. Whoever built this structure clearly mined a lot of underground tunnels to source enough blocks to build.

INVENTIVE DETAILS

I've restored many ancient mechanisms in my time, but never anything as dangerous as this gravel trap. I quickly learned to tread carefully around the ruins after a misstep nearly sent me to my grave.

GRAVEL TRAP

My ancestors were clearly doing their best to protect their possessions when they built this. The enormous gravel trap uses signal ladders, redstone dust and sticky pistons to unleash a whopping 150 blocks of gravel upon whoever disturbs the pressure plates that line the bridge. A gritty way to go!

BANYAN ALTAR

Upon ascending the stairs to the altar room, I was immediately set upon by undead mobs. As I fought my way in, I saw why: There were mob spawners everywhere! The redstone mechanism that controlled the lighting was damaged. I quickly fixed it and put a stop to the undead onslaught.

COMBINATION DOOR

After avoiding the gravel trap, I came across a combination door. It took a while, but I solved the sequence and recorded how it was constructed.

INSTRUCTIONS

Use the step-by-step images provided to create your own combination doorway. I redesigned the entrance to use three sticky pistons to open and close it. It's a complicated mechanism, so make sure you follow the steps carefully.

2

Extend the support structure upward as shown.

1

Start by creating the base of the support structure for the automatic door mechanism using lime terracotta.

3

Place three deepslate bricks on the left and three polished blackstone blocks on the right.

180°

8

Place levers on each of the deepslate bricks and polished blackstone on the front of the build to activate the piston doorway.

180°

9

Finally, create a facade for your entrance. This structure uses blocks such as deepslate gold ore and candles to give a decrepit effect.

7

Create a tunnel using chiseled blackstone.

4

Create a signal ladder using redstone torches. Then place some redstone dust, 2 redstone torches and a redstone repeater on the support structure as shown.

6

Build the entrance using lime terracotta, gold blocks and chiseled deepslate.

5

Place two slabs with redstone dust on top of them, then place three sticky pistons attached to deepslate blocks.

COMBINATION

In order to open the gate, you need to flick the levers into the right combination. Only when the redstone signal reaches the sticky pistons will it open.

THE PATHFINDER

Welcome aboard! We're blazing a trail out in deep space on *The Pathfinder*, a fully self-sufficient solar-powered intergalactic space station, which proves that the sky really is the limit for our ambitions. This behemoth will help us discover new worlds, encounter new peoples and expand our technology to the farthest reaches of the universe.

RING ROOMS

COMMS ROOM

HYDROPONICS CENTER
This is where all our food is grown.

ROXY ROCKET
ENGINEER

GRAVITY CONTROL

CONTROL BRIDGE
This room controls every function in the station.

SOLAR POWER STATION
The engine is powered by renewable energy sourced from over 80 solar panels.

PROPULSION JET
The primary thruster jet for moving the station.

DIRECTIONAL JETS
These secondary thruster jets are for turning the ship.

AIRLOCKS
For technicians to get in and out of the station to conduct repairs.

EXTERIOR

My station has rotating ring rooms and uses gravity-control mechanisms to create artificial gravity in each wing of the ship, so they can work in isolated harmony.

RING ROOMS

RELAXATION SPA
Being out in space for years can be stressful. The engineers come here to relax and get a sense of home.

HYDROPONIC FILTERS
Water is filtered and repurposed through the hydroponics center.

GREEN SPACES

AUTOMATIC FARMS

SOLAR PANELS
Countless solar panels harness the power of the sun.

INTERIOR

INVENTIVE DETAILS

My space station is full of technology to aid the crew. For instance, each wing of the ship is connected to a set of solar panels to ensure life-support systems continue to run in the case of malfunction.

CONTROL BRIDGE

The control bridge is the most important room on the ship, as it is where we can manage the entire station. The three control modules are used to monitor the vital support systems, from hydroponics and gravity to engine power. It requires a crew of hundreds when at full operation.

RADIANCE

The sea lanterns around the hull of the spaceship illuminate *The Pathfinder* in space.

COMMS

These antennae allow us to communicate with our team back home. We transmit all our latest discoveries.

ENGINE

The engine is a powerful beast capable of traveling thousands of blocks per second.

LOUNGE

Even the hardest of workers need some downtime. The lounge is the perfect place for the crew to relax and chat about their day.

RING ROOMS

These special ring rooms use a unique rotating wheel design that automatically turns to keep the rooms level. The water at the base of the ring helps sensors know when to rotate in order to maintain the artificial gravity.

CAPACITY

The ring rooms are enormous, with enough space for hundreds of astronauts. Each ring contains over ten floors and countless rooms.

INVENTIVE DETAILS

Our long voyages make it almost impossible to store enough fresh food to keep the crew fed. That's why I built a series of automatic farms – my crew are far too busy to worry about producing food as well!

ENGINEERING

The walls of the station are packed with redstone engineering. These redstone power lines allow us to control everything from emergency doors to lighting and even the toilets from the control bridge.

HYDROPONICS

Central to our farming system is the hydroponics room. Here we grow kelp, berries and melons to keep the crew sustained.

BLOCK CHOICES

Traveling out into the endless void of deep space exposes the station to many threats – space debris, atmospheric pressure and freezing temperatures. This ship is built out of durable material to keep it safe.

white concrete

orange concrete

gray concrete

gold blocks

iron bars

54

BERRY FARM

Sweet berries are an excellent source of vitamin C, an essential food for preventing scurvy outbreaks aboard the ship.

KELP FARM

Kelp is a fast-growing food source, making it an ideal crop in limited space. It can also be used as fuel, so if our engines ever need more power, we can use kelp blocks to keep them going.

AIRLOCK

Airlocks allow for crew members to step in and out of the station to conduct repairs. They must go through two sealed gates to ensure the station's vacuum isn't disrupted.

KELP GROWTH

When the kelp grows, the observer activates, triggering the piston, which cuts it down to size. The kelp then floats to the top for collection.

MELON FARM

Melons are perfect for our farms, as one stalk can produce an almost infinite number of melons. I used an observer above and a piston to automatically harvest the melons when they're fully grown and a minecart to collect them. What's more, glistering melon slices can be used to create Potions of Healing in case any crew member gets hurt.

SOLAR POWER STATION

These solar panels are the primary source of power on board the ship. A series of 80 panels capture the power from stars to fuel the engine.

MEEPLE PARADISE

Where are we? We're in my bedroom, of course! My world is a perfect replica of my bedroom . . . except everything is far bigger. It's filled with all the funnest games, but getting around can be a little tricky. I've packed my inventions into all the nooks and crannies — see, there's even one in the desk drawer! If only my real bedroom was this awesome!

INDOOR GARDEN

PARKOUR WALL
To reach the top shelf, you need to journey up the parkour wall.

MODEL BUILDS

SATURN V ROCKET

DRAWER MAZE

JOURNAL MONUMENT

MIKE ROSCOPIC
MEEPLE DESIGNER

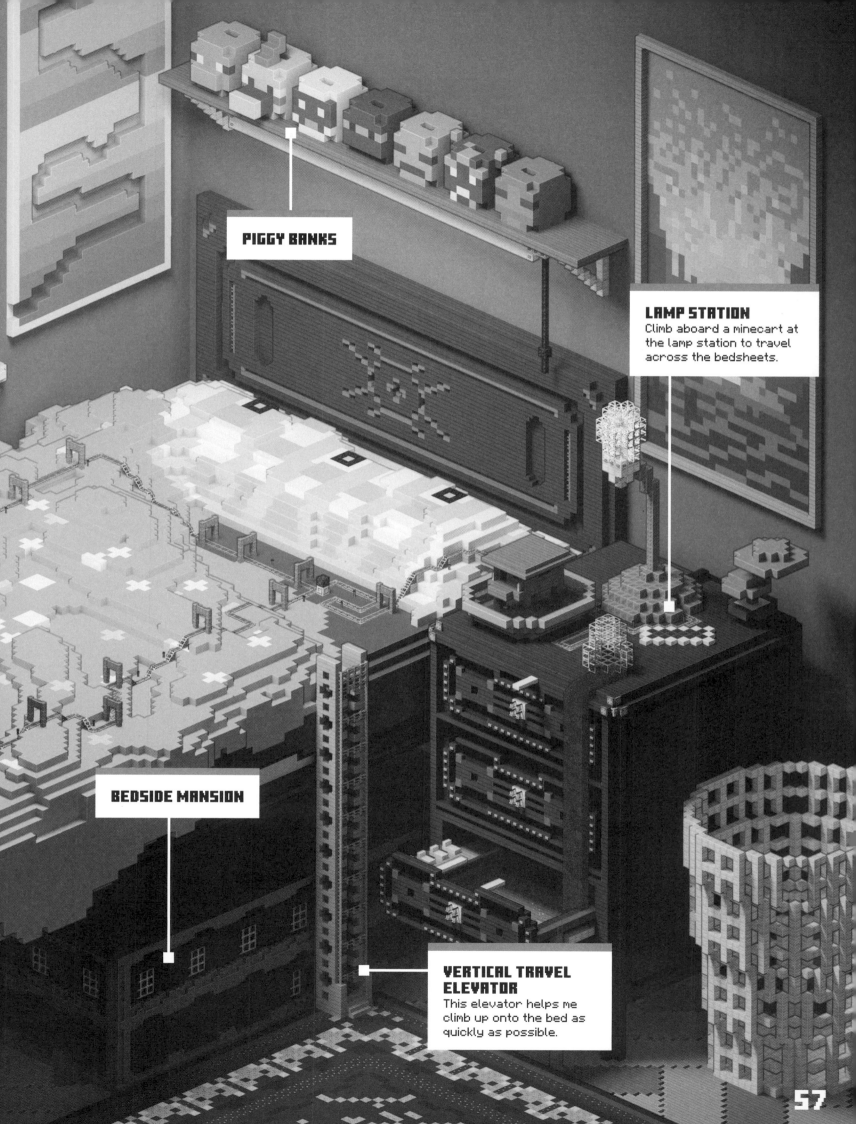

PIGGY BANKS

LAMP STATION
Climb aboard a minecart at the lamp station to travel across the bedsheets.

BEDSIDE MANSION

VERTICAL TRAVEL ELEVATOR
This elevator helps me climb up onto the bed as quickly as possible.

57

INVENTIVE DETAILS

My room is my space, so I have filled it with all my favorite things. I constructed the model builds and Saturn V rocket myself! I put them on the shelf on full display. And I have the best collection of piggy banks.

AQUARIUM

I built an aquarium using glass blocks. It's filled with kelp and coral, and there are even some decorations for the fish to play around in.

PIGGY BANK COLLECTION

I love to collect piggy banks. I have one for each of my favorite mobs: pigs, chickens, sheep, Endermen, skeletons, foxes and zombies. They all have trapdoors underneath, so I can empty them.

CREEPER TOY

A big cuddly creeper toy! It's made with the softest green and gray wool, and the bubblegum is made of pink wool.

LAPTOP

Okay, okay, this isn't a real laptop. But it's the same as the one I have in my bedroom! It's where I play Minecraft.

BONSAI

Bonsai are small trees that are specially trimmed as they grow to stay small. This is an acacia bonsai I've been trimming for years.

VILLAGE

Better clean up under your bed or you never know what will start to live down there! Like the entire group of villagers that have moved into my model village.

CALENDAR

I record all the most important dates on my calendar. There's only one truly important date this month – MY BIRTHDAY!

BLOCK CHOICES

My bedroom is full of life, so I used lots of bright colors to build it. The bed is made with the softest wool I could find, and all the furniture is made of wood.

light blue wool

yellow wool

green concrete

glass

dark oak planks

SATURN V ROCKET

My very own rocket! The *Saturn V* rocket was originally built to take astronauts to the moon. This rocket is made of concrete, iron bars and buttons, with cauldrons for the jets and lightning rods for the nose.

INVENTIVE DETAILS

My bedroom has all the coolest stuff – trains, posters, piggy banks, you name it! As it's all meeple-sized, I made lots of inventions for getting around quickly. See if you can spot them all.

DRAWER MAZE

You can reach my desk by making your way through the drawer mazes. Each drawer has a labyrinth you must explore until you find the staircase to take you to the next level.

POSTER RUN

I converted my rainbow flag into a running mini-game for scaling the wall. It's not the fastest way down but it's certainly more fun than jumping!

PARKOUR WALL

Hop, skip and jump your way up the wall to reach the indoor garden. Careful you don't fall – you don't want to find yourself tumbling down the side of the bed.

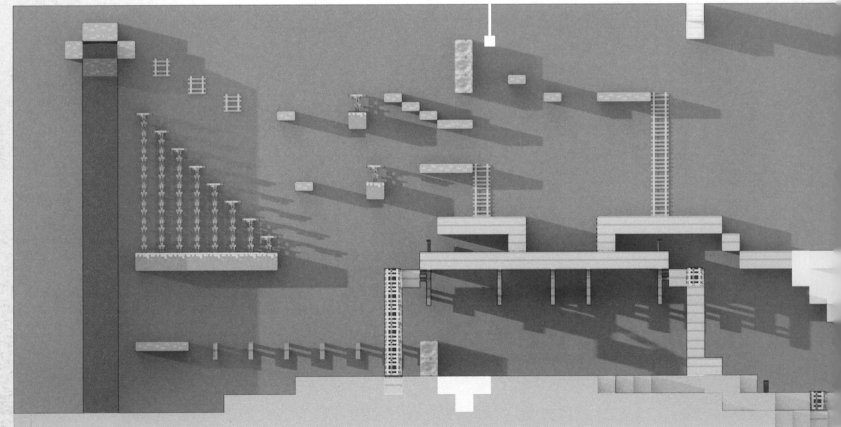

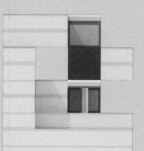

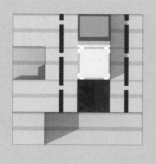

VERTICAL TRAVEL ELEVATOR

The quickest way to get onto the bed is by using the vertical travel elevator. Place a redstone block at the bottom of the elevator and jump on – the pistons will carry you to the top.

SECTION OF THE ELEVATOR

LAMP STATION

Make your way up the nightstand to reach the lamp station. Here you can catch a ride across my duvet to all the top destinations – check out the journal monument, visit the indoor gardens or make your way to the maze drawers. Just hop into a cart and the powered rails will take you on a journey.

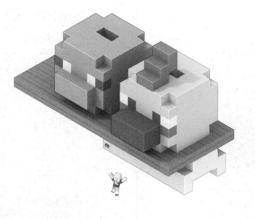

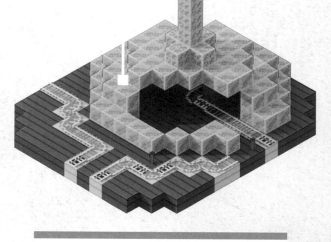

BOUNCY PILLOW

I love jumping on my bed. It's just so much fun, I had to include it here on the pillow. Climb up to the piggy bank shelf and jump from the chicken beak to bounce super high on the slime blocks below.

SKULL MOUNTAIN

Welcome to my island! Before we continue, you must first swear to secrecy. There is more to this island than meets the eye, and under no circumstances can the other expert inventors become wise to my nefarious plans. Muahaha! That's right – where their inventions are for the curious and the good, mine focus on realm domination! Beneath the surface lies my secret villain lair.

SUN LOUNGERS
My fellow inventors often visit for a holiday. Little do they realize what is hidden beneath them as they sunbathe.

ISLAND DOCKS
The secure docks protect yachts from the occasional tropical storm.

SKULL MOUNTAIN
This mountain gives the island its namesake – it looks exactly like a skull!

DR. NEFARIOUS
EVIL MASTERMIND

FIRE PITS
Spots on the beach allow my resort guests to spend their evenings with songs and marshmallows!

PAVILION
These resort buildings hide the true nature of the island.

You've seen my cover resort, but now it's time for me to show you the real beauty of this island: my secret evil lair! No one will suspect that within the mountain, hidden beneath the very skull it is named after, I'm hiding a TNT rocket!

LIBRARY OF WICKEDNESS
This library is full of the most gloriously evil books. I come here to find inspiration for my wicked deeds.

CREEPER FARM
This is where I farm creepers for their gunpowder.

TNT ROCKET
My rocket is hidden where no one will think to look for it.

DORMITORY
Evil lairs require workers and workers require beds! Though only for a few hours – I want them at their grouchiest!

PLOTTING ROOM
Even evil villains have meetings to plot their dominion.

INTERIOR

In my secret villain lair, I have constructed training grounds for my troops and gunpowder farms for my realm-destroying weaponry. Above ground, I have built things to keep my resort guests occupied – and distracted!

MARTIAL COMBAT TRAINING

In order to take over the realm successfully, it is essential that my troops are better trained than any other fighters. I put them through arduous training exercises to improve their skills.

TNT ROCKET

If my nefarious plans should ever backfire and my lair is discovered, then this rocket will transport me far, far away. It's loaded with enough TNT to blast me up to the stars.

SHOOTING RANGE

I don't want to draw any unwanted attention, so my shooting range is also hidden in the lair. My troops practice their bow and crossbow aim in this secure room. The iron bars keep stray arrows from injuring anyone.

SKULL SILO

There's more than meets the eye to this skull! – in an underground chamber beneath lies my TNT rocket! When the time comes, the skull will split in two, revealing the rocket beneath, and I will begin the launch countdown for my crafty escape.

FIRE PIT

Who doesn't love toasting marshmallows over a fire? I needed something to draw in paying guests to the resort to fund my villainous plans.

DOCKS

We don't want anyone flying overhead and spotting anything suspicious, so this island is only accessible via boat.

sand

gray concrete

white concrete

dark oak planks

stone

smooth quartz slab

BLOCK CHOICES

As my base serves two functions, island resort and villainous lair, I've used a variety of blocks. It has everything from warm sand to cold, sturdy concrete.

INVENTIVE DETAILS

My invasion won't get very far without gunpowder, so I have built a creeper farm to gather plenty of it. To make sure no one has figured out my plans, I've got sneaky ways of keeping tabs on them.

HIDDEN DOOR

The entrance to my secret lair is accessible only by a hidden iron door, which is controlled by a comparator. In order to open the door, a book must be placed on the lectern, activating a comparator that sends a redstone signal to the iron door.

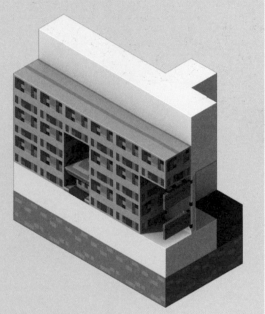

CREEPER FARM

This creeper farm spawns and defeats creepers to collect their drops automatically. Build this farm to gather all the gunpowder you need.

INSTRUCTIONS

Follow these steps to build your very own creeper farm. It can be built above or below ground, as no light enters the build where the creepers spawn.

1

Build a 25x20 base for the farm. Include a large chest with 2 hoppers as shown. This will be the collection room.

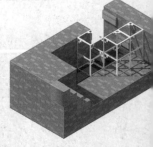

2

Add 2 layers of stone blocks, leaving a gap in the structure.

3

Place 6 glass blocks around the hoppers to close the passage. Then place 2 signs on both sides of the passage as shown.

10

Add finishing details to your creeper farm. Place iron bars around the borders and iron trapdoors on the roof. Add a staircase leading down into the collection room.

9

Add another layer of gray concrete and iron blocks.

8

Seal the chamber with a dark oak trapdoor roof.

7

Extend the gray concrete walls by 2 blocks and place orange carpets as shown. This will be the spawning chamber for the creepers.

4

Place 2 lava sources alongside the glass blocks, then place 2 water sources at the end of the passage. This water will carry the creepers toward the lava to be defeated and their drops collected.

5

Build another layer of blocks on top, adding glass blocks over the long opening and leaving a hole over the end of the water for the creepers to fall through and another for access to the chest.

6

Add a 13x16 layer of gray concrete and iron blocks in a butterfly formation, and add oak trapdoors around the hole in the center.

CHAMPION ROOM
Make your way to the Champion Room to collect your rewards!

STATUE
The name of every Diamond Maze victor has been inscribed at the base of the statue.

DIAMOND ROOF
The angular glass roof of my building shines like a diamond in the sun and gives the maze its name.

SEA LANTERN MAZE

PUZZLE ROOMS
There are dozens of puzzle rooms, each with hidden chests for you to find.

PER PLEX
GAME SHOW HOST

DIAMOND MAZE

Do you want to play a game? Step on up to the Diamond Maze! This build is a game show and I'm your host, Per Plex. The rules are simple: Start at the bottom and make your way to the top. Your goal is to complete the puzzles on each floor and collect redstone torches to reach the Champion Room. The more puzzles you complete, the greater the rewards!

ASCENSION TOWER
The ascension tower awaits you at the end of the maze. Climb up to reach the Champion Room.

ENTRANCE HALL

WATER FEATURES
Water fountains add elegance and beauty to my build's surroundings.

EXTERIOR

CHAMPION ROOM
This room is full of reward dispensers for the champions.

UNDERWATER CAVERN
Take a deep breath! These rooms are completely submerged underwater.

DESERT CHAMBER
This oasis can play tricks on the mind. Solve it quick!

CACTI CANYON
Watch you don't get pricked by these cacti! Move carefully but quickly – find the chest and get out of the room before you get locked inside.

JUNGLE PUZZLE
Listen very carefully. There are a dozen mobs here and you need to guess which ones – without seeing them.

The Diamond Maze is designed to test your mental and physical abilities. Each room will pit you against a new biome and new puzzle. I hope you know your Minecraft lore – you're going to need every scrap of knowledge to win.

NETHER RUN
I hope you know how to tame a strider, you're going to need their help to get across this room.

INTERIOR

INVENTIVE DETAILS

In Minecraft, diamonds shine blue, and so does my angular roof! Every block in this build screams of luxury, from the countless gold and emerald blocks to the rich blue stained glass and delicately chiseled sandstone.

SOUL CAMPFIRES

My build looks incredible at night, with all these alcoves dotted around the roof, containing soul campfires. Even in the dark, you can spot my spectacular building from many blocks away!

EXTERIOR BLING

If you need proof of the wealth to be won within, look no further than these decorative rings at each end of my building. They are made of emerald and diamond blocks — no expense was spared!

ENTRANCE HALL

Before beginning our game show, contestants gather together in the entrance hall. You'll have a moment to discuss one another's strengths before starting your journey together.

LEVEL END

Each floor of my maze has many rooms. Completing each room will activate a dispenser in a rewards room, where contestants will go at the end of each floor to collect redstone torches, which they can exchange in the Champion Room for prizes.

BLOCK CHOICES

I chose my blocks to make my build look rich and reminiscent of diamonds. Blue-colored blocks are prevalent throughout.

blue stained glass

warped fences

diamond

soul campfire

STATUE

This red sandstone statue stands tall outside the maze. The diamond blocks in its hand entice players to try their luck in my game show.

ASCENSION TOWER

There are multiple routes through the maze, each leading to one of four ascension towers. You can choose to exit to the Champion Room at any of these, but if you stick around and venture deeper into the maze, you can collect more redstone torches and earn greater rewards.

INVENTIVE DETAILS

As you make your way through the maze, you'll need to complete a series of rooms. I have come up with many puzzles to put your problem-solving skills to the ultimate test. You'll need to be quick too – some rooms will lock you in if you take too long!

ELYTRA LAUNCHER

After ascending to the Champion Room and collecting your rewards, you and your team can exit the Diamond Maze in style. Walk over to the elytra launcher and fly out to the thundering applause of a fireworks show!

180°

RIDDLE CLUE

Keen-eyed players will take note of the pillars beside the lever puzzle. The fence posts provide a clue as to how many levers need to be pulled.

LEVER PUZZLE

Solve the redstone riddle to complete this puzzle. There are 6 levers that must be switched in the correct order to open the door and reveal the chest.

TIME LOCK

I've built this fancy time lock using hoppers and a comparator to control how long players have for each puzzle. The circuit uses hoppers to create a timer, which will eventually trigger the lock when the last one is full. The timer length can be adjusted by moving the final repeater closer or farther away from the comparator. Once time runs out, it will close the door and lock you in if you're not finished!

1

Switch the lever to pull the sticky piston. This will activate the redstone torch, unlocking the hoppers and starting the time-lock countdown.

180°

3

Once the central hopper is full, the comparator will send a signal to reach the repeater and lock the circuit, meaning time is up for your players!

2

The hoppers will pass an item back and forth to create a clock circuit. Each tick of the hopper clock will send a pulse to the second group of hoppers, which will slowly fill up the central hopper.

REWARD DISPENSER

Every room you complete will reward you with a redstone torch to activate a reward shrine. Placing the redstone torch in the space below the dispenser will activate it to give you your reward.

BATHHOUSE

WATER ELEVATOR

MOUNTAIN CORRIDOR
This passage is the
only safe way down
the cliffside, and leads
to farms far below.

TOPSY TURVY
AERIAL ENGINEER

HANGING VILLAGE

Whoa there, don't look down! This is not a place for those scared of heights! Just take a moment to find your feet, this hanging village is dizzyingly high. It's perfectly safe, don't you worry. I'd avoid jumping around though, unless you're wearing a handy elytra – there are no safety nets to catch you if you fall over the edge.

SUSPENDED HOUSE
This home offers the best view in the village!

FORTRESS
This is the village's largest and grandest building, tucked into the corner of the cliff overhang and defended on all sides by the rest of the village.

LANDING PAD
This is the entrance to my village, but you can get there only by flying in by elytra with fireworks to boost you up. I placed water beds to prevent injuries upon landing.

This village is built just like any other, except everything is upside down! The top floor is the new ground floor, and the ground floor is the new penthouse. These village residents have the most astonishing view in the realm.

HANGING TOWER

These hanging towers are the main structures in my village. They get gradually narrower and narrower, and the floors are connected with ladders. Sentries keep a lookout through the trapdoors, which they can open to defend against assailants.

LANDING PAD

Flying around with an elytra and fireworks can have you moving at very fast speeds – fast enough to hurt with a crash landing! I built these landing pads with water beds to absorb the impact and avoid any fall damage.

BATHHOUSE

The bathhouse is the only building I built not dangling upside down. There are two rooms on every floor, each offering a spa treatment: hot baths, ice-water pools, mud baths, saunas and steam rooms.

MOUNTAIN CORRIDOR

I dug caverns into the mountain wall to provide additional space for storehouses and access to the mines below. It also features an escape route through the mountain – just in case!

BLOCK CHOICES

My build is defined by its prismarine eaves. The layered, tiled roofs give the structures depth, and the blue-green prismarine allows my village to feel at one with nature in a magical way.

dark prismarine stairs

dark oak logs

flowering azalea leaves

red sandstone walls

SUSPENDED HOUSE

Though not the largest, this home hangs lower and farther out than any other building. It's connected to the mountain arch by a chain of anvils, providing the best view of the surrounding area.

FORTRESS

I built the fortress at the heart of the village as it is the social hub for the residents. Without any ground to roam around on, these rooms provide entertainment and open spaces for lounging.

INVENTIVE DETAILS

etting to and moving around this hanging village can be a little tricky – there's not always an easy footpath between buildings. I've created an elytra launcher for visitors to access the village, as well as a few unique travel corridors to help move from room to room.

SPIRAL STAIRCASE

Though basic, this spiral staircase is the safest way to move about these houses. If you run out of fireworks to propel you in the right direction, or if you miss your stop on the water elevator, you can take the stairs. It'll take longer, sure, but you'll get there eventually!

BRIDGE SUPPORTS

All the dangling houses in my village are connected by bridges to allow the inhabitants to move around freely. These bridge supports act as crossroads and junctions between buildings, allowing me to create multiple levels of bridges, while also providing the narrow walkways with the support they need to stay aloft.

WATER ELEVATOR

This water elevator allows for vertical travel between floors. A soul sand bubble column pushes players up the elevator on one side and a magma bubble column pulls players down on the other side. I've used trapdoors and signs to avoid flooding.

MESSAGE TRAIN

A railway runs from the ground to the top of the mountain to carry messages. The hopper collects the messages and they are then brought to me in the fortress.

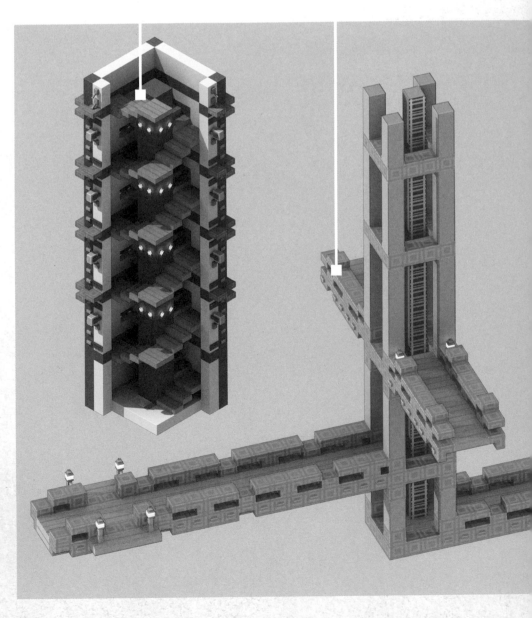

ELYTRA & FIREWORKS LAUNCHER

The quickest way to move around the village, and the only way to reach the village in the first place, is by elytra, with fireworks used to launch you in the right direction. Only expert flyers should attempt to travel from room to room this way – the entrances are narrow and if you miss, the drop is lethal.

INSTRUCTIONS

Using the images provided, follow the steps to build your very own elytra launcher. This contraption should be built on the ground to launch you into the sky.

1

Build an 8x6 concrete base for your launcher.

2

Add 5 more concrete blocks on top in a Y formation, then add a sticky piston a block above it.

3

Place 2 redstone torches facing outward on the 2 singular blocks, 3 redstone repeaters – 1 to the left of the sticky piston and 2 on the concrete Y as shown. Then add a ring of redstone dust around the outside of the left side, connecting the repeaters.

4

Add another 3 concrete blocks above the Y as shown and a slime block on the sticky piston.

5

Place a stone pressure plate and 2 more redstone torches on the latest concrete blocks, then position an observer facing downward on the left as shown.

6

Place 3 crying obsidian blocks in a V formation around the pressure plate.

7

Place 3 more concrete blocks – 2 on top of the redstone torches and 1 above the observer.

8

Place another sticky piston with a slime block as shown and then 2 dispensers above the obsidian blocks and fill them with elytras and fireworks.

9

Finally, encase your launcher with decorative blocks. I used stripped warped stem, acacia and dark oak blocks for mine.

90°

83

SURVIVAL ARENA

Are you quick or strong? Smart or nimble? You'll need to be all of them to enter my arena and make it out alive. Inspired by the Roman colosseums of old, my arena is full to the brim with games I have invented in order to weed out the weak and find the strongest players in the realm. Step forward if you dare – winners will be greatly rewarded. Those who fail will pay the ultimate price.

ROUND 2: NETHER
The winning team then advances to the Nether arena to battle their way through hordes of mobs.

GLADICE ATOR
GAMES MASTER

REWARDS
Chests full of useful items are on top of each tower.

ROUND 4: ESCAPE!
Once you have completed all of the rounds, a portal will activate, allowing you to leave.

ROUND 1: EARTH
First, you step into the Earth arena. This is a melee battle where two teams are pitted against each other.

ROUND 3: OCEAN
Any contestants left standing will then move on to the Ocean area where they must parkour up the towers and retrieve an elytra from the chest.

INVENTIVE DETAILS

Step on up and I'll explain the challenge. There are four rounds to the arena, each game more dangerous than the last! The final round will pit you against a surprise boss, so the more players who make it to the end, the greater your chances of survival.

ROUND 1: EARTH

The Earth arena is for the PVP battle. The barren arena is littered with obstacles and traps, so watch your step! One false move and you'll find yourself falling into a pitfall.

ROUND 2: NETHER

The Nether arena is a hostile zone, with lava and magma blocks to sap away the health bar of any inattentive contestant. Battle your way through mobs to reach the Ocean arena.

ROUND 3: OCEAN

The Ocean arena is a large parkour course. You'll need to time your jumps perfectly to make it across. If you fall, you'll need to make your way back to the beginning and start again.

ROUND 4: ESCAPE!

Upon completing the Ocean round, all competitors must make their way to the center of the arena where an escape portal will have activated to carry them home with all of their rewards.

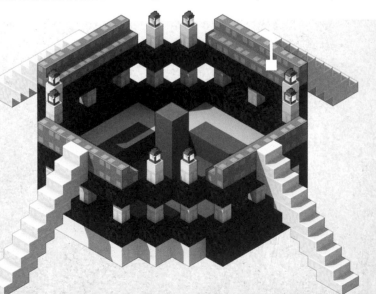

GRANDSTAND

The arena is open to spectators. Hundreds of players can watch as contestants make their way through the games. Spyglasses are provided so that everyone can keep a close eye on the action.

ARMING CHAMBER

Before you enter the arena, you'll have the opportunity to choose your equipment for the games. There are six sets of weapons available for different styles of fighting. Choose wisely!

DUELING TOWERS

Each area features tall obsidian towers that players can climb. The exposed facade leaves you vulnerable to attacks, but chests on top contain items to help you advance.

INVENTIVE DETAILS

Each game features unique traps and pitfalls. I've designed these to test the mettle of every player. Once triggered, you'll have to think fast and react faster to stay one step ahead of the challenge.

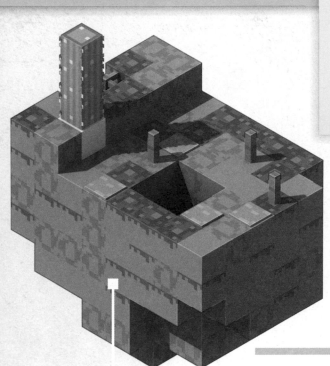

NETHER SPAWNERS

The Nether round is littered with dozens of mob spawners. These spawners will send a continuous stream of blazes, zombies and skeletons to attack contestants until they are all destroyed.

CACTUS AND PITFALL

Watch where you jump! Crashing into a cactus will take away your health bar, and falling into one of the pits will leave you trapped until the mobs overrun you.

AUTO ARMORER

When you respawn after battle, you're going to need to rush to get back into the fray. I built this auto armorer to have you re-equipped in seconds!

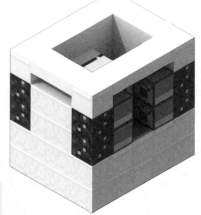

TNT TRAP

Simple but powerful, this pressure plate will trigger TNT blocks that will quickly eliminate any players who linger around too long.

SINKHOLE

Watch for strong currents in the Ocean games. Magma blocks create bubble columns that will pull you to the depths of the water and burn you if you get too close.

podzol

water

coarse dirt

End stone

BLOCK CHOICES

Each arena is themed, with blocks chosen to fit each one: Earth, Nether, Ocean and End.

SAND TRAP

There are pressure plates scattered all around the first round. Some will cause the sand around them to fall, plummeting you into a pit of mobs – including powerful piglin brutes!

INSTRUCTIONS

Using these steps, build your very own sand trap. Once finished, place them around the arena at random intervals, so that your competitors keep on accidentally falling into them! Mix up the mobs you place in them to keep your contestants guessing!

1

Dig a pit in the ground 6 blocks deep and 5x5 blocks wide.

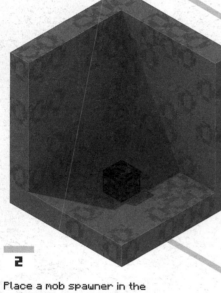

2

Place a mob spawner in the middle of your pit and click it with the egg of the mob you want it to spawn.

3

t ground level, place a olid block with a pressure late on top of it. Then lace a downward-facing iston beneath them and dd another solid block nderneath.

4

Build a layer of signs coming from the lowest block, covering the whole pit. You'll need to crouch to place a sign on another sign.

5

Place 2 layers of sand blocks on top of the signs, surrounding your pressure plate.

6

Surround your trap with decorations to make it look unassuming and distract your contestants from the pressure plate.

GOODBYE

And there you have it! You've reached the end of the tour around the Creator's Realm. I must say, even I'm amazed! We engineers can sometimes have our heads in the clouds – or space, in my case – as we invent and figure out ever cooler builds, and we often don't know what everyone else has been making. It's been great to take this tour with you! I can't wait to use their ideas in my next galaxy-spanning project! I'm not sure what I found most useful, Gladice Ator's nifty auto armorer or Topsy Turvy's ingenious vertical travel elevator. I know what I'm doing tonight – I'm going home to see what I can create with redstone now that I've seen how my fellow experts do it!

What about you? Do you have an idea you want to explore? If you're unsure where to get started, why not try out some of the build guides within these pages, and when you're done, see how you can improve them.

I'm afraid it's time to bid you farewell. The sun's setting and we must all get back to our builds before Dr. Nefarious gets any ideas while we're all distracted. So go get inventing and maybe someday we'll be visiting your realm for a tour of your epic inventions!

FENRIR'S TOOTH

Welcome aboard my ship, *Fenrir's Tooth*! These decks have taken me across the deep blue seas, from the heart of civilization to the farthest and darkest corners of the realm. Armed with a veritable arsenal of artillery, we bring the fight to the mobs and banish evildoers from the land. Keep an eye on the horizon and listen for the sound of the cannon announcing my arrival.

WOLF HEAD
Strike fear into the hearts of your foes with an intimidating figurehead.

BRAZIERS

GUNHILDA FENRIR
Viking Berserker

CROW'S NEST
Always keep an eagle-eyed ally
posted in the lookout box to warn
the crew about imminent threats.
The drowned know no peace.

FLAG

EMERALD WOLF

ARTILLERY CANNON
A watery grave awaits the poor souls facing
this powerhouse. If you thought creepers were
explosive, you haven't been introduced to my
TNT-fueled friend.

OARS

EXTERIOR